ABC

Construction Vehicles Book

I0528791

AO PRESS

Jessica Lee Anderson

Paperback ISBN: 978-1-964078-02-1

In memory of Paul Nordstrom, a grandfather with much knowledge about a variety of vehicles and a tool for everything. -JLA

Note that vehicle names have been capitalized for emphasis.

Photo credits—Front cover: A: Andyqwe (Dump Truck), B: uatp2 (Bulldozer), C: JoLin (Concrete Mixer Truck), Photochecker (Bulldozer), agnormark (Road Roller); Back cover: Roger Brown (Backhoe Loader); Cover page: A: Andyqwe, B: uatp2, C: JoLin, Baloncici (Boom Lift), jondpatton (Excavator); Copyright page: rcphotostock; Dedication page: supertruper (Front Loader); p. 4: Ocskaymark, Industrial Photograph; p. 5: uatp2, no_limit_pictures; 6. Kozmoat98, zhanglianxum; p. 7: mladn61, Juan Jose Napuri Guevara; p. 8: alexmak72472, jean52photostock; p. 9: kozmoat98, TA2O4NORI; p. 10: poco_bw, Chinnasorn Pangchoeren; p. 11: mladn61; p. 12: sirene68, Sergiy1975; p. 13: Jordi C, peuceta; p. 14: Lex20, Maksud_kr; p. 15: Naypong, Dusan Bartolovic; p. 16: Daniel Mazilu, Philipp Berezhnoy; p. 17: Cineberg, aluxum; p. 18: ewg3d, Sjo; p. 19: Maksim Safaniuk; p. 20: germi_p, Anze Furlan; p. 21: Ivan Smuk; p. 22: Industrial Photograph, kadmy; p. 23: NiseriN; p. 24: Joe_Potato, Christine_Kohler; p. 25: MikeVanSchoonderwalt, AlekseySagitov; p. 26: orthogon; p. 27: uatp2, anmbph; p. 28: Mungkhoodstudio's Images, luamduan; p. 29: Baloncici; p. 30: stefann11 (Agricultural Tractor); p. 31: Michael Anderson

This Book Belongs to:

_____

is for Asphalt Paver

Asphalt Pavers lay asphalt (also known as blacktop or bitumen) for paving projects like roads, parking lots, and walkways.

B is for Bulldozer

Bb

Bulldozers dig, clear land, move materials, and level the ground, plus they can do other things like plow snow or tear up asphalt.

C is for Concrete Mixer Truck

Cc

Concrete Mixer Trucks mix materials like cement, sand, gravel, and water that then will exit out of a chute for projects like buildings and roads.

**D is for Dump Truck**

D d

Dump trucks have large buckets in the back of the truck that are used to load, move, and dump materials such as rocks and dirt.

 is for Excavator

E e

Excavators have a bucket, an arm, a rotating cab, and wheels or tracks so that it can dig, lift, and do other things like drill holes or break down walls.

**F** is for Forklift

F f

Forklifts have an attachment called a fork that is used to lift heavy objects and move them short distances.

G is for Graders

Gg

Graders have a long blade that flattens and levels surfaces at places like mines, construction sites, and farms.

is for Horizontal Boring Machine

Horizontal Boring Machines drill sideways to lay pipes or cables—some machines are large enough to bore tunnels!

 **is for Impact Hammer Excavator**

Ii

Impact Hammer Excavators have a breaker that loosens compact soil and drills into hard materials like rocks.

J is for Jackhammer Excavator

Jj

Jackhammer Excavators are just like Impact Hammer Excavators, and they come in a variety of sizes—they smash rocks and can be used to open areas for pipes and wires.

K is for Knuckleboom Loader

Knuckleboom Loaders are a type of swing machine that load and unload various types of cargo (like logs) in tight places.

L is for Long Reach Excavator

Long Reach Excavators feature an extra-long arm that can be used for hard-to-reach projects and to demolish buildings.

 is for Manlift

Manlifts are also called aerial lifts—they help to lower and raise workers on a platform to get them where they need to be.

 is for Night Light Tower

Portable Night Light Towers and lights on cranes keep a construction area well-lit at night so workers stay safe.

 **is for Off-Road Dump Truck**

Off-Road Dump Trucks (sometimes called Articulated Dump Trucks) are heavy-duty trucks that have a special joint which allows them to move around on all kinds of surfaces.

P is for Pipe Layer

Pipe Layers lift, carry, and place pipes in the ground, an important task when it comes to creating water, sewer, and utility lines.

P p

 is for Quad Axle Dump Truck

Quad Axle Dump Trucks have a fourth axle which adds strength and allows these trucks to take on longer and heavier loads.

**R** is for Road Roller

R r

Road Rollers (sometimes just called Rollers) are used to build roads or foundations by compacting soil, gravel, concrete, or asphalt.

21

S is for Skid Steer Loader

S s

Skid Steer Loaders are compact vehicles often used for digging, and they can do many other tasks like trenching and clearing snow.

 T is for Telehandler

Tt

Telehandlers are like a combination of a crane and a forklift—they carry heavy goods from place to place using crane-like prongs called a boom.

U  is for Utility Truck

U u

Utility Trucks are like workshops on wheels as they carry tools and equipment for repairs and maintenance work.

V  is for Vertical Tower Crane

V v

Vertical Tower Cranes have a part called a lifting boom that is used to carry heavy loads up to staggering heights!

is for Wheel-Tractor Scraper

Ww

Wheel-Tractor Scrapers are used to move and remove earth—they have a pan/hopper for loading and carrying materials.

 **is for X-Shaped Scissor Lift**

X x

Scissor Lifts can carry multiple workers at once, and when the lifts extend, their scissor legs make X-shaped patterns.

Y is for Yard Crane

Yard Cranes raise, lower, and lift heavy objects in container yards or other places like a construction company's yard.

is for Zipper-Like Chain Trenchers

Zipper-Like Chain Trenchers have a metal chain with teeth-like parts that can tear into soil, tree roots, and even asphalt.

5 Construction Vehicle Facts

1 Construction vehicles play an important role in creating buildings all around the world.

2 Construction vehicles move a massive amount of dirt, rocks, and other debris that would difficult to do otherwise.

3 Dump trucks are some of the most common construction vehicles. The first ever dump truck was invented over 100 years ago!

4 Heavy-duty vehicles play a big role in farming and mining as well as in construction.

5 Construction vehicles improve productivity, safety, and efficiency at work sites.

Jessica Lee Anderson is an award-winning author of over 75 books for young readers. Jessica lives near Austin, Texas with her daughter, Ava, and husband, Michael. Watching cranes go up and down was one of Ava's favorite pastimes when she was younger. You can learn more about Jessica by visiting www.jessicaleeanderson.com.

Check out these other titles:

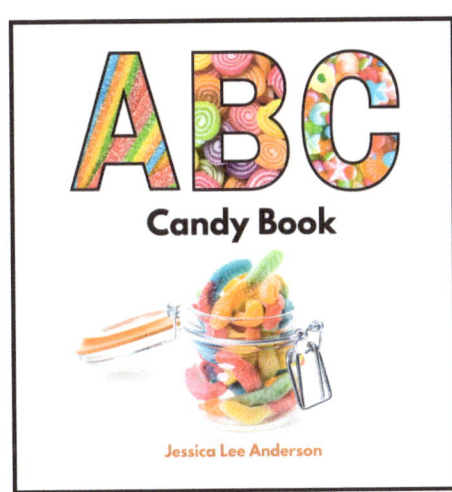

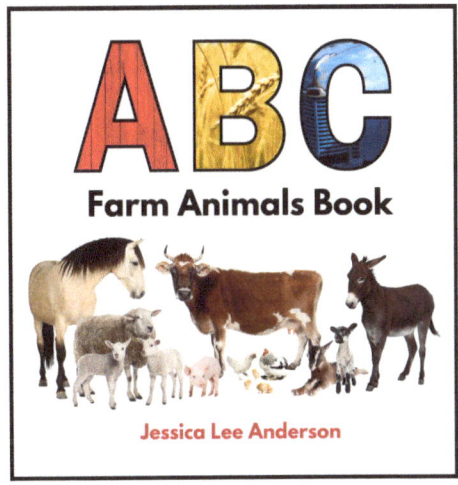